W9-DDY-449

SPRING IS LIKE THE MORNING

Spring, for the outdoor growing world, is like the morning. It is a time to wake up and a time for new things to happen. It is a time to use your eyes and to use your nose and to use the tips of your fingers. Every day there is something new to smell, to hear, to feel.

But spring does not go on forever. It goes into summer and summer brings fall, then winter, and sleep. Next year, though, there will be another spring and it will be like the morning.

spring
is
like
the morning

by M. Jean Craig / illustrated by Don Almquist

G. P. Putnam's Sons / New York

It has been cold outdoors for days and days and weeks and weeks and months. You wear your heavy coat when you go out to play, and your fingers need mittens or pockets to keep them warm.

It is still a little bit dark when you get up in the morning, and it is dark again before you sit down for supper.

Some days are sunny, but often the sky is cold and gray. You look up at it and you shake your head wisely and say, "I think it is going to snow again tonight."

There are no flowers in the garden, no green leaves on the trees. There are very few birds, and no butterflies or bees at all. In the yard, the earth under your feet is as hard as a wooden floor.

When you walk across the brown fields or
into the bare woods, there is nothing to hear
but the wind. Everything else is very, very quiet.
It is so quiet that you think the outdoor world
must be asleep.

You are right — the world really *is* sleeping. It is sleeping because it is winter, and for all the outdoor growing world, winter is a kind of night.

But it has been winter now for much too long, you think. You are tired of the cold and you are tired of the short days and you are very tired of your heavy coat. You almost wonder if it will go right on being winter forever and ever. (You know, of course, that it never does. But it feels as though it might, doesn't it?)

And then, one day, along comes a day that is not the same as other days at all. Sometimes this happens early in the year, in March. Sometimes it is a little later, in April. Whenever it is, you can tell right away that it is not like a winter day at all.

When you go off to school in the morning you forget your mittens. But your hands are not a bit cold holding your books.

The air feels warmer and softer against your face than it has felt for days and days and weeks and weeks and months.

Your nose doesn't get red and runny when you play ball in the back yard after school.

The sunshine feels different, too. It has been bright and hard during the winter months. But today it is warm — warm and soft, like the air.

If there is snow on the ground, it begins to get slushy. As it melts, some of it makes puddles, but the rest soaks down into the hard earth. Then the earth becomes soft, too.

On this day that is not the same, everything seems soft and different — the air, the sunshine, and the earth. It is so different that you think the outdoor world must be waking up.

And you are right — the world really *is* waking up.

This day that is different is the first day of spring. And spring, for all the growing world, is a time to wake up.

Spring, for all the outdoor growing world, is like the mornin

19

Spring is a time for new things to happen. You can see some of these new things happen and you can hear some of them happen. Some of them you can smell, and many of them you can feel and touch.

Spring is a time for you to use your eyes and your ears, your nose and the tips of your fingers. If you use them well, you can learn about the growing world as it wakes up.

When spring comes, everything new does not happen at the same time. Nothing new happens until it is exactly the right moment. And the right moment is only *after* something else has happened first!

Do you know the very first sign of spring? Of course you do — you noticed it the day you left your mittens home. The weather is *warmer*. And this is why:

Every morning in the spring the sun comes up a little earlier than it did the morning before. Every evening it sets a little later. As the spring goes on, therefore, each new day has more minutes of sunshine-time.

And something else is changing, too.

In the winter, when the sun is low in the sky even at noon, the sun's rays slant across the earth like this:

But in the middle of each new spring day, the sun is a little higher overhead than it was the day before. In the spring, the sun's heat and light strike the earth more directly.

Because of this, the sunshine feels warmer than it did in the wintertime. These longer, warmer hours of sunshine are the real beginning of spring. It is the spring sunshine that melts the ice and snow. It is the spring sunshine that makes the hard earth soften. Without the soft wetness of the earth there would be no spring at all for the growing world, because everything that lives and grows on earth must have water.

You can see the longer days of spring with your eyes, and you can feel the warm air and sun on your skin. You can touch the wet, soft earth with your fingertips, and you can smell it, too. Even before you can see anything beginning to grow, the earth has a growing smell in spring. And the new growing of everything that lives is the next thing to happen in the spring.

The sun's heat and the wetness of the earth wake up the plants first. Hard, dry seeds, made by the plants last summer, have waited in the hard, cold ground for many months. Now they become damp and soft, and the baby plants inside swell and stretch. Tiny new leaves push up through the earth to the sunshine. Tiny new roots reach down for water.

Plants that already have roots, like bushes and trees, draw water up into their stems and under their bark. The tight buds on their bare branches were made at the end of last summer, too. Now the water in the plant stems — called sap — soaks into the buds. They stretch and swell like the seeds, until the bud coverings crack open.

Pick one, and carefully take it apart with your fingers. You will see the shape and the color of the new leaves and flowers that are beginning to form.

While the buds are opening, bright new grass blades spring up between the old dull ones on the lawn.

In your garden, the kind of plants that grow from bulbs begin to poke their noses up out of the ground.

In the woods, you can find young ferns
curling up from the dead leaves under the trees,
and other early plants.

Almost as soon as anything at all begins to grow, the very first spring flowers open, too. The very first spring flowers do not look like what we usually call flowers. Often they are small, and their colors are not always bright. Pussy willows are really flowers. (Are you surprised to learn this?) There are flowers on most trees, such as oaks and maples and birches, that look like little wings, or fuzzy balls, or long tassels. They are really flowers, even though they do not have pretty petals or a very sweet smell.

But most spring flowers are bright and glowing and soft in the bright, soft sunshine. Many burst from their buds even before the leaves are out. How many of these early spring flowers do you know? Do you know which ones grow wild, and which must be planted in gardens?

Your nose will tell you which ones smell sweet and which ones hardly smell at all.

As soon as the plants are wide awake and growing fast, the buds and the stems and the leaves become green and juicy. Then a great many more things happen very quickly, one after another.

All insects feed on plants or on other insects that feed on plants. Did you know that? In the winter, there is nothing for them to eat. So some insects sleep all winter — deep in the earth, or under the bark of trees, or in little nests they have made of mud or leaves, or in the corners of buildings.

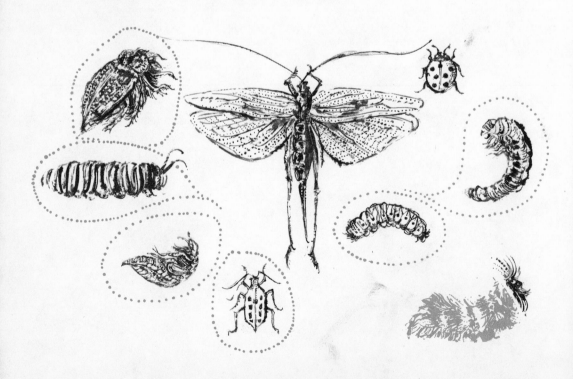

Some insects spend the cold months in little cases, until it grows warm enough to hatch out into a true insect shape.

But when they feel the spring sun, out they come, all of them.

Out they come, just exactly when there is sap flowing again in plant stems for them to suck, and young fresh leaves for them to chew, and flowers with nectar and pollen for them to drink and eat.

Now the woods and fields are no longer quiet, as they were in the winter. Now there is a buzzing and a humming to hear. There is a fluttering and a darting and a crawling that you can see. The insects know it is spring and so do you, because you can hear it and see it and smell it and feel it, as they can.

When you hear and see the insects, you know it is time to listen and watch for the next sound and sign of spring. For once the insects appear because food is ready for them, the spring birds fly back from the South because there are now insects for them to eat.

Suddenly, one morning, you will see a robin on the grass, hunting for worms. A thrush whistles at you from the edge of the wood, and a towhee scrabbles in the leaves under the mulberry tree. There goes a barn swallow — did you see it? And wasn't that a yellow warbler? You can see and hear them all, if you look and listen in the right places.

There are other animals that eat insects, and if you live near a pond or a brook, you will surely hear one of them, too. It makes one of the first spring sounds — and one of the very, VERY loudest! If you hear a shrill, chirpy whistle that goes on and on and never seems to stop, you are listening to the song of a tiny frog only this long:

It is called the spring peeper — of course! It has spent the winter deep under the icy mud. Now that the mud is soft in the sunshine, the peeper has climbed out into the air again. It sits near the edge of the pond or stream, and just about every minute that it is not catching insects it peeps and peeps and peeps.

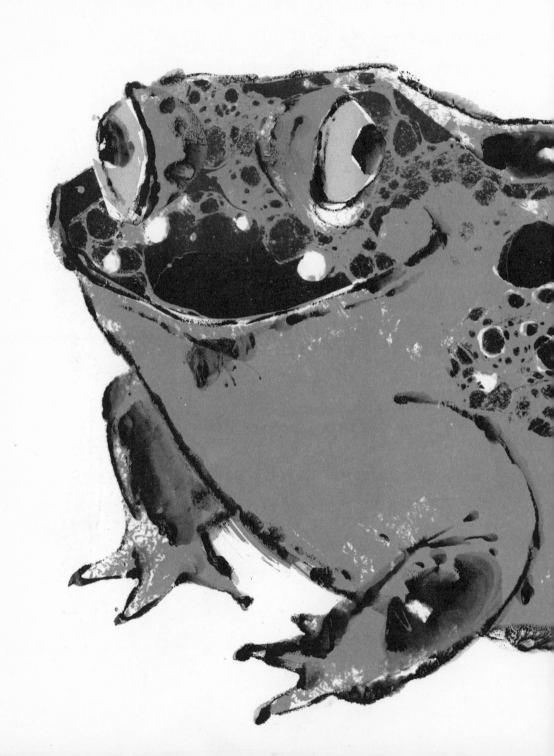

The other, larger frogs — the ones that croak deep in their throats — also wake up from their winter's sleep in the mud. Perhaps it is the noisy peeper that wakes them.

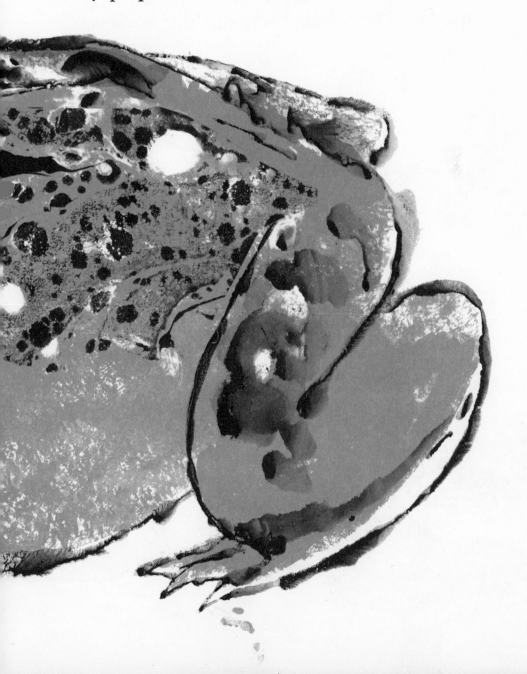

The slow turtles climb up onto stones and logs and lie in the sun all day. They are not so slow after a few sunbaths have warmed them up. Walk near them, and you will see how quickly they splash back into the water.

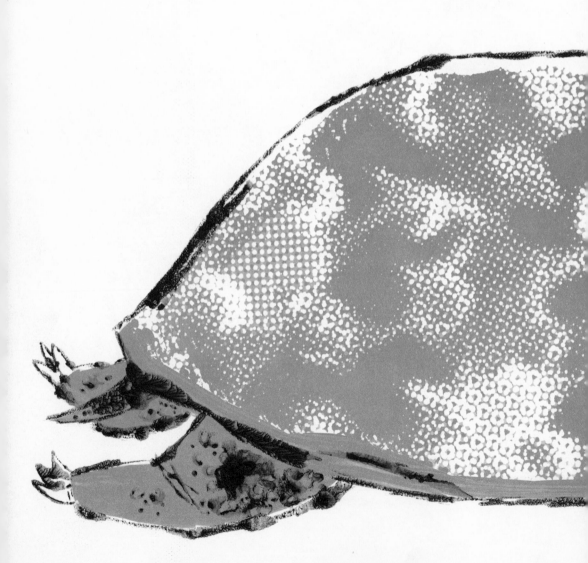

And by now the furry animals that have slept all winter are awake and ready for their breakfast — and their lunch — and their dinner!

Many of them have new babies. There are big bears and small bears, fat old woodchucks and chubby little new ones, mama chipmunks and tiny young ones. And all of them are HUNGRY.

Deep in the woods the baby deer are born, just when the oak leaves have become large enough to hide them from spying eyes. The rabbits and the mice and the moles have brand-new families. They are all eating and eating and eating, so that they can grow quickly.

The birds race to build their nests, lay their eggs, and then feed and raise their babies. The bees are gathering nectar from the flowers, to make honey for the young bees in the hive and more honey to store for next winter. They zoom back and forth, back and forth, between the pink-covered apple trees and the white clover blossoms in the meadow.

Everything is in a hurry in the spring. Everything grows faster in the spring than at any other time of the year. Later, in the summer, the sun may be too hot, instead of just nice and warm. And often, in the summer, there is not much rain. There is enough rain in the spring — almost always.

There are many short, hard showers, and
sometimes there are days when the rain falls all
day long, soaking steadily into the earth. Rain
and the warm sun — the warm sun and then
more rain — this is spring.

As the days grow longer, and the outdoor growing world becomes green and rich and lovely, you wish that spring would last forever. Every day there is something new to see and to smell, to touch and to feel and to hear. Every day there is something new to learn.

But the winter did not go on forever, did it? And neither does the spring. Spring is a wake-up time for the growing world, and by the time the world is *wide* awake the spring is over, and it is summer.

Next year, though, there will be another spring, and you can learn more.

And there will be another the year after that, and then another, and another.

Just as the morning always comes after the night, spring always follows the winter. Spring will always come, year after year after year, until the end of time.

The Author

M. Jean Craig has worked in the fields of public opinion analysis and sociological and biological research. SPRING is her first book for Putnam but she has to her credit three other juvenile fiction works: *The Dragon in the Clock Box, Boxes,* and *What Did You Dream?* Miss Craig makes her home in New York City.

The Artist

Don Almquist, a graduate of the Rhode Island School of Design, has appeared in practically all the magazines at one time or another — either editorially or via the advertising page. The recipient of a number of awards and citations, he has done several children's books. He and his family are presently living in Sweden.